How I Got Free Stuff To Sell Online and Quit My Job!

…You Can Do It Too!

Paula C. Henderson

[How I Got Free Stuff To Sell Online And Quit My Job]

DEDICATION

This is for everyone who has a dream.

[How I Got Free Stuff To Sell Online And Quit My Job]

CONTENTS

ACKNOWLEDGMENTS

I want to acknowledge my Dad who believed girls could do anything boys could do.

Paula C. Henderson

1 MY BACKGROUND

I wanted to share a little background about myself. Not everything of course but my business background. My work experience. I've had some pretty interesting jobs along the way leading up to my online business.

My first job ever was babysitting like so many tween age girls. But my first real job, for an employer where I paid taxes was walkin' beans and detasseling corn. If you grew up in rural Illinois in the seventies you know what I am talking about. I was in junior high and in the summer we would all meet downtown on Main Street in front of the grain elevators to catch a bus that would take us out to the fields. Yes. Those huge sprawling fields you see when you are driving down the highway.

Soybean fields get weeds like any backyard garden and we would essentially weed the fields. They gave us a hook and we each had two or three rows on either side of us. We spread out and started on one end until we ended up at the other end of the field. Detasseling corn was different. They had a tractor or combine with a metal pole out each side with say four to six seats on either side. We sat on the seat and as the tractor slowly went down the row we pulled the tassel off the corn as we went by each stalk. Not fun work. It was definitely work. Very hot. Very humid.

When I started ninth grade I started working at my father's car

3

dealership. He owned a Ford Dealership. My mom worked in the office. They moved me around where they could use me after school and on Saturday mornings. I filed dirty, oil smelling parts invoices, learned how to use an adding machine, a typewriter, count money back to the customer and that sort of thing. I also spent many the afternoon standing behind my father's chair in his office and listened to him talk to Ford, customers, and the auctions on the phone. Making deals, negotiating. Leading his salesman. Conducting meetings. Dad also did television commercials for the business. It was fun seeing my dad (otherwise a very stressed grumpy moody man) do these silly commercials. One time he popped out of a peanut for a sale he had coming up. The slogan was something like; Jerry's gone nuts! Another time they made it look like he was sitting on this gigantic bunch of bananas with the slogan that he'd gone bananas slashing prices.

My first real job after graduating high school was in a funeral home. I answered a classified ad to sell caskets and funeral packages door to door. I was provided with one of those large binders with full size color photos of caskets. Thank goodness that didn't last long. Just a month or so in and they ask me if I would be interested in working in the office. Yes! Yes I would.

This was an interesting business. So there was a cemetery just outside of town. A beautiful sprawling cemetery. And this guy from Chicago buys it. Moves down to Tennessee, where the cemetery is. He buys a single wide trailer and puts it in the middle of the cemetery. The outside still looked like a regular white single wide house trailer, but on the inside he converted the living room into the front office, the master bedroom became the funeral parlor if you will (where we held the actual funerals), and the second bedroom was the office I worked in. They did add on one room to the back, off the office for performing the embalming's.

Lesson here? Just start. Start where you are. That is what I learned from this. Personally I would have been embarrassed to ask people to have their loved ones funeral in a single wide trailer but guess what? It worked. We were very successful. The owner did what he could afford to do to start his business. He let his intention to help people at one of their most difficult times be the selling point.

In the beginning the owner did all the landscaping and mowing, met with families helping them arrange the funeral for their loved ones and with the assistance of one hired experienced grave digger helped dig the graves and then assisted with the process of the burial after the graveside services.

That was in the mid-eighties. That funeral home is still in business but now the funerals are conducted in a beautiful brick funeral home they were able to build some ten years after he started. He was patient. He believed in what he was doing and the products and services he offered. My grandmother passed away a few years ago and they did a wonderful job on her funeral service.

While I working at the funeral home I took an H&R Block tax course and worked part-time at H&R Block preparing taxes for a couple of years. From there I was told about a slaughterhouse that was opening and they needed an office manager. This seem like a step up so I applied and got the job. I learned a lot working at the slaughterhouse.

Did you know that when a cow is taken to slaughter (our customers were places like grocery stores and fast food restaurants that needed beef) the cows hide is removed, spread out and any cysts, tumors and moles were removed, put in an igloo ice chest, taken to the bus station and sent to a Cancer research lab. Not sure what they did with it but it made for more interesting work for sure. I also found out that they removed the penis of the bulls and were sold to some company that used them to make walking canes. Seriously. You cannot make this stuff up.

In 1988 my father asked if I would move to Columbus, Ohio to help him start a new business. I did. It was a fleet disposal company. Our company contracted with companies like Hertz, banks, Kraft Cheese, etc. These companies leased most of their company cars and trucks. At the end of the lease they use a fleet disposal company to pick up their vehicles, value them, and pay them for them. The fleet disposal company has a couple of options: take it to a vehicle auction and sell it, or place it on a used car lot for sale with a used car dealer they have contracted with.

This company continued regular success until my father's death in 2002 and continues today by his partners. He started this company with the $77.00 he had in his savings at the time. I worked for the company from 1988 through 1992. At the time I left, still in its infancy the owners were each drawing a salary of $2000.00 weekly.

Again, start with what you have. Start with what you know. Don't get me wrong; Dad certainly did not know how to run the entire business. He hired people who knew what he did not so that he could focus on what he did best which was negotiating the price and purchase of each vehicle.

In 1992 I left there and took a course to become a Certified Weight Loss Counselor and got a job at a local weight loss center. I enjoyed the work. Learned a lot!

I went to a Temp Agency and took their typing and 10-key speed and accuracy test. That landed me a few jobs over the course of the next few years: I worked at a chiropractor's office filing insurance claims. Worked in dispatch for Pepsi. And, I worked as a transcriptionist for the county parole office which landed me some freelance transcribing gigs with the private investigators. Which lead me to calling the local vocational school and letting them know I was available if students were looking for people to type up resumes or papers.

It was around this time that our local library was getting renovated and they were adding an addition to the back. A really big project. I wondered if they paid someone to clean up the construction mess inside. I ask a couple people I knew; "wonder if the construction company pays people to clean up the mess they make inside". They laughed at me. Told me, no they just clean up after themselves.

For some reason I could not get it off my mind. I felt compelled to find out so I bought a clipboard, grabbed a pen and stopped in one day. Found one of the construction guys who pointed out the foreman. So I ask him. "Do you have anyone hired to clean up?". He said, "no, take a look around and give me a bid". Okay. So I walked around. Not sure what I was looking for or even at. I noted there were a lot of windows that would require a ladder. A big ladder. A lot of marble flooring. Lots of old beautiful woodwork. I ask him if I could drop off a bid on Friday and left.

I didn't even own a ladder. Other than a step ladder that was two feet tall I think. I knew nothing about marble or cleaning windows. I got the local newspaper and called a couple of classified ads I found for window cleaning services and some for general cleaning. They gave me quotes based on the information I gave them. I added 20% and typed up a quote which came to $2400.00, thought up a business name, went to the courthouse and applied for a vendors license ($15.00 at the time) and dropped the bid off on Friday. He called me a few days later and said I got the job and to make sure I brought proof of insurance before starting to work on the property.

So I called the guy I had my car insurance with and told him what was going on. He advised me on what I needed and let me set up monthly payments to get insured. I was in! How exciting! I called back the window cleaning company and four of the cleaning ladies I had found in the paper.

We all had a meeting. The job went well and the contractor ask me to then give him a bid on a bank renovation they were doing in another town about 30 miles away. We did that and then a Taco Bell, a McDonalds, a Mexican restaurant, many residential houses along the way. I had called the newspaper and ask them how much a standing ad in the classifieds section would be. Leave it in every issue of the paper bill me monthly. We were getting calls left and right. We were travelling over a 100 mile radius. We were on our way. Then I used some of the money and had 500 brochures of our services printed up and sent them out to all of the contractors in the area.

We got one call. But that call was for a contractor that worked with a developer that built entire subdivisions. So a winning bid with him was guaranteed work for the next 3 years over the course of building 250 houses in a golf course subdivision. We got the job. I ended up buying a couple company vehicles and having several different crews.

The thing to note is that one thing can lead to another. You have to start somewhere and you don't need to know everything to jump in. You just have to understand that you cannot pretend to know and then possibly do a bad job. Always keep a good reputation for yourself and your business. Hire people who do know how to do the work properly. Rely on them.

I had my cleaning business for 10 years. It was ten good years. For health reasons I moved to the southwest and this business model did not work the same out here. It was 2003 and times had changed. The internet was the next big entrepreneurial thing to do.

2 JUST A DREAM

Just A Dream

By 2003 Ebay was all that. Selling online was a dream of many. It has been for a long time. Sitting at home in front of your laptop. In your pajamas with a cup of coffee. Sounds nice, doesn't it?

The big question seems to be what to sell. Seems that if you could answer that question you would have the world by the tail.

My experience, that I am about to share, taught me one very important lesson: Don't try to predict what someone will pay good money for. Seriously. Some of my biggest money makers were things that made no sense to me. If you get stuff free and you have time to list it and the room to store it then my advice is to list it at least for a time. Or put it in your yard sale. Whatever format you use to sell products.

EBay seems to be the big selling market of used stuff. I did sell there but I made my most money by selling used products on Amazon. I listed stuff where it made sense. Where I thought it would sell. You will get a handle for that as you go along. If you already sell online you already know what sells better where. I had the occasional yard sale too. Just to clear things out and then I may take things to Goodwill and donate what was salvageable

9

but no good to me. The rest I threw away.

Now you don't necessarily need a lot of room. If your thing is small stuff like jewelry, coins, lids, then you may not need much space. If your thing is books, DVD, CD's, you will need a good size room with bookshelves. Clothing; room for racks and a mannequin is a great thing to get for pictures. Be sure you are prepared to throw things away and drop lots of stuff off at the nearest goodwill store or church thrift shop.

This is not just a good method for gathering items to sell. This can also help you if you sew or do crafts. A great way to get buttons, material, yarn and other supplies you may use to make your handmade goods that perhaps you sell on Etsy.

Many people don't realize how much stuff thrift shops throw away. Trust me, most of them would rather not throw anything away. But they are inundated with donations and sometimes simply cannot keep up, don't sell enough of it or just don't have the space. If you are a charity and need clothing this is a good place to look!

I'm getting ahead of myself! I did not make handmade crafts, sew, paint or have the money to invest in inventory. Year after year went by and I would hear about others who had quit their jobs and were selling online. I wanted to do that too! It sounded perfect.

Then I tore a ligament in my knee. Now this sounds like a bad thing and I will admit it was very painful. I had surgery and then I had about a month of rehab time where I was stuck in bed pretty much most of the day for at least that first week after coming home. I was not to return to work for 4 weeks. What to do?

3 THE IDEA

The Idea

I found myself in bed with not much to do but think, read and surf the internet. I once again found myself trying to come up with that one brilliant idea I needed to start my own online business. I thought back to a business I had in Ohio in the nineties.

When I had the cleaning business I would get calls from realtors and individuals who needed a house cleaned so they could put it on the market. A house left by someone due to foreclosure or death. So it was full of belongings that had been left behind. They told me to do whatever I wanted with the items in and around the house; just make sure it was empty and clean so they could list it for sale. I donated quite a bit of stuff but I also found things worth selling. I got to know some of the thrift store owners quite well and found out they get a lot more stuff donated than they have space for and they do not like throwing it away.

One day it just came to me. I wonder if the thrift shops and second hand stores would be willing to let me pick up what they were just going to throw away. I could re-donate some items to other thrift stores in the area and charitable organizations that needed donations and sell the more valuable things to cover my costs and create a job for myself. Recycling at its best.

My first thought was the same that many of you are having right now. Why would you want garbage? If it's sellable the thrift stores would most certainly keep it and sell it.

Well, actually, no.

I wrote up a letter and mailed it out to every Goodwill store, thrift shop and secondhand store in the area and I also put an ad in the local newspaper. The jest of the letter and the ad was that I would pick up your unwanted items for free. No Charge. I added a footnote to the letter stating I would not pick up obvious garbage; i.e. broken items, unknown bags of items, and no Encyclopedias or readers digest books.

The first thing I found out is that the Goodwill stores were not interested. Someone from one of the Goodwill Stores called me after receiving my letter. They explained that they would never have an overflow of donations because they just ship it to other Goodwill Stores in the state.

Good to know. I did appreciate the call. I made a point of just mailing letters or calling locally owned thrift shops, hospital and church thrift shops.

I was pleasantly surprised by the response. Within a month I had 3 stores that emailed me in response to the letter and stated they always had so much more in donations than they had room for in their store, or the manpower to deal with, and hated to throw perfectly good items in the trash.

They ask if I was willing to just schedule a regular weekly or biweekly pick up date. Well yes! Yes I was!

4 EXPANSION

I also put an ad in the newspaper.

The ad in the newspaper was free. Our paper had a classified section at no cost to place an ad if you were offering something for free. I ask if they could place the ad and leave it in each issue so long as they had room. They said sure.

I would receive calls from the newspaper and shopper ads about once a month. Usually people who were moving. Or after a yard sale.

The ad: WILL PICK UP UNWANTED ITEMS. NO CHARGE. PLEASE CALL: XXX-XXXX

Then I started getting calls from area realtors from the classified ad in the newspaper. The realtor calls were great bump in business. It was always because a homeowner had walked off and left an entire household full of stuff behind. Usually because the house had gone back to the bank. So then I went with that and sent out a second round of letters to all of the realtors in the area.

I was well on my way with regular pickups weekly and one monthly from the three thrift shops that had responded originally. A realtor call for a big job approximately every two to three months, and the occasional response from the newspaper ad from either individuals or many times a business.

I had one thrift shop in particular that had way more donations of books, DVD's, and music CD's then they had room for in their little store and that monthly pick up would fill my car. When I say fill it I mean from top to bottom and I could not take anyone along because I would not have room for them to sit once I crammed everything in the car.

Another thrift shop had piles of clothes. The good thing was that a lot of it was new with tags. When they told me they received more donations then they could handle they were right. These were piles of clothing they had not had time to go through. Meaning I was not picking up the scraps after they had picked through it. I was picking up fresh donations. So a lot of good stuff. Now I won't lie, you have to be prepared to throw many items in the trash and I also donated a lot of stuff to my local church thrift shop and Goodwill store that I did not pick up from.

Don't make the mistake of donating to a thrift shop you pick up from. It is highly likely you will just pick it right back up on your next visit. So donate those items to local charities looking for clothes, or Goodwill Stores and other places you don't have an arrangement with for pick up.

The realtors brought on a landslide of items and spawned a sort of second business. We finally ended up buying a small box truck. People walk away from these houses sometimes leaving what seems like everything. Furniture, silverware, appliances, clothing, books, electronics, bicycles, patio furniture and so on. Anything you find in and around a house.

I also worked out a small payment from the realtor to take care of emptying the house (not cleaning it) but emptying so they could bring in cleaning crews. The realtor would pay me between $200 and $400 depending on the size of the house and I would make sure the house was empty and ready for the cleaning crew. I generally would go through everything very quickly at the house and set the trash out at the homes curb. Then I would call the local trash company for a one time pick up and have them bill the realtor. Then I went home with all the items I thought I could sell.

Without having to buy any of it and many times getting paid to pick it up!

5 IS THIS FOR YOU?

Before you decide to go for several thrift shops, and a couple of realtors, you might want to ask yourself a few questions:

Are you willing and do you have the time to sort through a lot of various items; a lot of which you won't want?

Do you have the room to store your new inventory?

Do you have the time to re-donate a lot of it to a different thrift shop or charities in the area?

Can you handle more trash than the average person?

You can certainly limit what you pick up if the thrift store is agreeable. Say you only want dishes, children's clothes, just electronics, or books. Simply say that in your initial letter to them. I have included a few sample letters that you are welcome to copy and use in their entirety or edit as you see fit.

I mailed a hard copy letter to the thrift shops and realtors I made contact with but if you feel you would get a better reaction using email, making a phone call or stopping by in person then try that. Do what you are comfortable doing.

If they want to know what you do with the items be honest.

Let them know you sort through everything and donate to appropriate thrift shops or charitable organizations that can use the items and that you sell the rest online to curb the cost. Do not donate back to the same store you picked it up from. I found that Goodwill was unwilling to let me pick up free items so I donated to them. There was also a couple of smaller church and hospital thrift shops in the area that did not respond to my letter of picking up free items so I donated to them as well.

You may want to consider looking into your areas charitable organizations and find out what their needs are. Most will keep a list of the items they need on their web site. So if you find you are more interested in selling knick knacks or jewelry at least you have a plan in place for the clothing. I would keep clothing with tags to sell but any other clothing, as long as it was in good condition, I would donate appropriately after researching who needed what. I would divide the men's, women's and children's clothing and donate accordingly once a month.

Thrift shops generally don't mind what you are doing with this free stuff they are giving you if they get a sense you are doing some good with it at your own expense and they in turn don't have to feel bad about throwing it in the dumpster or turning it away.

I included a couple of thrift shop sample letters at the end.

If you purchased my little booklet to get some ideas I hope you feel you have.

I enjoyed my time selling online. It offered me a good steady stream of income while working for myself. It was a nice balance of working at home but also getting out in the community.

Coming home with a car load of free product was exciting. While sorting through items I had brought home never knowing what I might find! Then settling in and spending the next week or so listing new items for sale while taking orders, and packaging for shipment.

It was a very busy but exciting time. You can keep it as small or let it grow as big as you are comfortable with. Hire someone to help you if you need to.

6 IN CONCLUSION

I still frequented yard sales and used book stores and bought items I felt I could markup a bit. And in the beginning, those first few years I was packaging all of my shipments and taking them to the post office. It took a while before the post office started picking up at my residence in the area I lived. If you don't have your packages picked up at your front door I highly suggest checking into it. It's free of charge and even if you enjoy getting out and going to the post office to drop your packages it's nice to have that in your back pocket in case you need to use the service at some point in the future.

Just go to the post office web site and on the main page you will see a link in the left column for

Scheduling A Pick Up.

It may or may not be available in all areas. I still use it today for personal packages. The post office will pick up all of your packages and letters at your front door through their scheduling system for free but they do require at least one of the packages be shipped via Priority Mail or Express Mail.

I am working on another book to elaborate more on sales techniques, shipping tips and online selling experiences I had with ebay, amazon and others as well as credit card acceptance and paypal tips I learned from experience.

If you follow my author's page on Amazon you will be notified when I release a new book. It is the only notification you receive when you follow an author so not to worry; you will not be put on any type of mailing list or anything. I actually personally have no way of seeing who, if anyone has followed my page but your support is very appreciated!

I wish you much success! (Don't forget about the sample letters to follow)

7 SAMPLE LETTERS

EXAMPLE 1 (change the wording to suit you and what you want to do and what you can accommodate)

Your Name, Your Address, City State Zip

Your telephone, Your Email

Date

Attention: Owner/Manager

Hello! My name is (your name). I pick up unwanted items at no charge.

I can pick up anything that would fit in a standard car. I do not own a truck so I would not be interested in larger items such as furniture. As you can probably assume neither would I be interested in obvious trash. But if you find yourself receiving more donations than you know what to do with and hate to throw these items away please feel free to contact me via (your preferred method).

I shop in your store on occasion and would love to stop by when you are available!

Regards,

(your name)

EXAMPLE 2

Your Name, Your Address, City State Zip

Your telephone, Your Email

Date

Attention: Owner/Manager

Hello! My name is (your name). I pick up unwanted books, music and movies at no charge to you.

If you find yourself receiving more donations than you know what to do with and hate to throw these items away please feel free to contact me via (your preferred method).

I sell what I can online to curb costs and donate the rest to clinics, charity organizations in the area and donate to a couple of church thrift shops.!

Regards,

(your name)

RESOURCES

Places to sell online today:

- Amazon: find a tangible product on amazon, say a book, a CD, a DVD or even a video game. Click on the Used for sale link under the correct option. Now you will notice in the center of the page next to the picture of the product it says: "Have One To Sell?" Click on that.

- Ebay

- Etsy

- Craigslist (find your local cities craigslist facebook page)

- Facebook: note from your personal page you can CREATE A PAGE. Start there.

This site: ecwid.com allows you about 9 products you can list and sell without any charge to you. They have the backend taken care of for you to accept payments and it allows you to connect it to your facebook page so you can sell on facebook. It's quite easy and they have good customer service if you need help.

Wix.com is pretty good (and free) if you want to build your own web site. They have a very user friendly shopping cart too.

A couple of tips I have found through the years:

- Allow customers to get to your product purchase buy now button with no more than two clicks.
- If you can name your links to your product listing pages be sure to use a distinct word that describes the product, not a catalog number.
- "Create A Page" on facebook for your product(s) store or business. If you are an author Create An Authors Page. A "page" unlike a group can receive likes. So as you friend people you can invite them to 'like' your page and when they do they see it and may just have a look around.
- Create posts on your business page and then share that post to your personal fb page. That way there is a link back to your business page where purchases can be made.
- Make sure all of your links are working. If they are not working remove them. Whether it is on your web site or social media pages. Nothing says unprofessional and you are not on top of things like a broken link to nowhere.
- Be clear about how you accept payment.
- Have a good clear picture of each product
- If you ship products always use tracking. Always.
- Never substitute a product without permission from the buyer. If they bought a red plate. Don't send them a blue plate.
- Utilize the USPS website. You can print postage and labels from there without a fee; just cost of postage and sometimes a discount for printing the label and postage online via their site. You can save your customers addresses in your account too. Go there and register and take a look around. You can also schedule a pickup of your packages for next day. They will pick them up at your front door. Very convenient and there is no charge for the service. Priority Mail flat rate is a cost effective shipping method. You can order your shipping boxes from their website. The boxes are free and they will deliver to your door. No shipping fees. Totally free.

ABOUT THE AUTHOR

Since selling stuff I got for free online I have also had an online business offering personal shopping that was quite successful. Scouring the popular shopping sites for products that were constantly out of stock but in demand. Then finding them in my local stores to buy and ship to the buyer.

Using my phone to take pictures of what seem like obscure products from my local stores. I would then go home and check to see if it was online for sale anywhere online. You'd be amazed how much is not available online but people want to buy online because either they are housebound or it is not available at the stores in their area.

Another niche was shipping to APO addresses, Alaska, Hawaii, Puerto Rico and Guam. Many sites use Federal Express and UPS only. And state they will not ship to these areas.

Using Priority Mail via USPS you can ship to these areas for the same cost as the next state adjacent to you. So I offered a service where if you found something on a site that does not ship to you I would order it, have it sent to me and the I would ship it to you. I charged a flat service fee plus cost of item and shipping. Lots of customers in Alaska!

What am I doing today?

Paula C. Henderson is a Nutritionist, Weight Loss Counselor and Author who makes her home in Las Vegas, Nevada. Creator of the 5pts Free Diet which promotes easing your symptoms from auto-immune, inflammation, depression, insomnia, obesity, hypothyroid, menopause, arthritis and more through diet and a healthy lifestyle.

Paula grew up in Illinois and then moved to Ohio where, as a single mother, raised her daughter.

Becoming a certified weight loss counselor started an interest in healthy food choices and a healthy lifestyle that continues today. Taking care of ones self is even more important when facing daily challenges. Through the years Paula has continued her education as a Nutritionist and health care advocate.

Paula has written several books on diet and nutrition. By following Paula you will get a notification as she releases each new book.

The 5 Points Diet Plan focuses on fresh foods you find in your local grocery store. Everyone is unique and this diet is customized to help you achieve optimal health and feel your best. #5ptsfreediet is dairy free, nightshade free, gluten free, soy free and grain free.

What's left to eat? That's exactly what the 5 Points Diet Plan shows you. facebook.com/5ptsfreediet

If you found this book helpful I would very much appreciate your leaving a review online: https://www.amazon.com/dp/B01KGP8FZU

You can find all of my books on Amazon (kindle and paperback) and my paperbacks are also available on Barnes and Noble.

Amazon authors page: www.amazon.com/author/paulachenderson

Outside of the United States search the ASIN or ISBN of the book you are interested in. You can find that on the authors page.

My paperbacks on Barnes and Noble: http://www.barnesandnoble.com/s/paula+c.+henderson/_/N-3